Understanding the
Roman Missal

The new translation

By
Dom Cuthbert Johnson OSB

*All booklets are published thanks to the
generous support of the members of the
Catholic Truth Society*

CATHOLIC TRUTH SOCIETY
PUBLISHERS TO THE HOLY SEE

Contents

Presentation

The Church in Britain and the whole English-speaking
world has a new translation of the Latin Roman Missal as
published in 2002 by Blessed Pope John Paul II. This
edition of the Missal contains the additional texts
approved by the Holy See during the previous thirty five
years. There are no changes in the Order of the
celebration of Mass.

Following the guidelines given by the Holy See in the
Instruction entitled *Liturgiam authenticam* the translators
have produced a text which has dignity, beauty and
doctrinal precision in a style suitable for Divine Worship.
The translation has been approved by the Bishops of the
English-speaking countries of the world.

This brief introduction to the prayers of the Missal is
designed to be more prayerful than technical. Excellent
works of catechesis have been prepared by the various
Bishops Conferences of the English speaking world
which will help make the introduction of the Missal be an
occasion for "a renewal and a deepening of Eucharistic
devotion all over the English-speaking world". (*Pope
Benedict XVI*).

Preparation for a sacred celebration

Recollection

All the great spiritual writers have insisted upon the need to cultivate silence and recollection. In the world in which we live with its distractions and noise, many feel the need for an oasis of silence and calm. Our churches can and should help to meet this need. In recent years the silence and recollection before Mass has been disturbed in some churches by unnecessary conversation both before and after the celebration of the sacred liturgy.

Even Saint John Chrysostom (347-407) had to remind the faithful of his time that "the church is not a barber's shop or a chemist's or a market stall; it is the dwelling of angels; it is the kingdom of God; it is heaven itself ... in the church, only spiritual things may be spoken, for this is heaven".

The church is our Father's house and the place where the community experiences its fellowship in Christ and should be a place where all are made welcome. It is possible to do this and at the same time not neglect that prayerful preparation which leads to a more profound participation in the celebration. Even Saint Paul had to remind some of the more exuberant members of the

Corinthian community that the character of the house of
God as a house of prayer must not be overlooked. Those
who have to prepare children and others for church with
all that this involves should not be anxious. All that is
done for love, even in trying circumstances, is for the
glory of God.

The church

To help our recollection we should remember that every
church building is an image of the holy city, the heavenly
Jerusalem, toward which we, the people of God, are
making our way on pilgrimage. As we enter the church
we should recall that we are passing from the world
wounded by sin into the world of new life which was
opened to us through our baptism. Taking holy water
reminds us of our baptism. As we walk through the
doorway we hear the Lord's words, "*I am the door; if any
one enters by me, he will be saved, and will go in and out
and find pasture*". *(John 10:9)*.

The altar

After an act of reverence to the Blessed Sacrament our
attention turns towards the altar on which the sacrifice of
the Cross is made present. The altar is also the table of
the Lord to which we have been invited. The altar has
been anointed with chrism and is thus a sign of the
Anointed One of the Lord, Jesus Christ, the victim, priest

and altar of his own life-giving sacrifice. The altar has been sanctified by the invocation of the Holy Spirit to become a visible sign of the silent yet eloquent witness to the saving work of our Mediator with the Father, Christ our High Priest.

The sacred character of the altar is expressed in this prayer from the Rite of the Dedication of an Altar: "May this altar be the place where the great mysteries of redemption are accomplished: a place where your people offer their gifts, unfold their good intentions, pour out their prayers, and echo every meaning of their faith and devotion."

The ambo

The place from which the Word of God is proclaimed is holy. The Fathers of the Church saw it as a throne for the word of God. The ambo is the table of the word and the seat of wisdom. The ambo holds up the Word of God as the altar and the sacred vessels hold up the body and blood of Christ. It is by hearing the word and sharing in the bread of life that we grow into the full stature of Christ.

The chair

Every celebration of the Eucharist is led by the bishop, either in person or through his priests. The Eucharist is the action of Christ and the people of God, hierarchically assembled.

The president's chair is a sign of his ministry of service in imitation of the Lord who came not to be served but to serve and give himself for us through his sacrificial death and glorious Resurrection.

The structure of the Mass

The fundamental structure of the Mass has remained unchanged from the time of the Apostles. The Mass is made up of two principal parts that form one single act of worship: the liturgy of the Word and the liturgy of the Eucharist.

The Mass begins with the introductory rites: the entrance chant and the veneration of the altar followed by the greeting, the Act of Penance, the Lord, have mercy, and, the Glory be to God (when prescribed). The introductory rites are brought to a conclusion by the Collect Prayer.

The liturgy of the Word is made up of Scripture readings, the homily, the Creed, (when prescribed), and concluded by the Bidding Prayers.

The Liturgy of the Eucharist begins with the presentation of the bread and wine. After the prayer over the Gifts, there begins the Eucharistic Prayer. The Lord's Prayer follows and during the Lamb of God there takes place the ancient and sacred gesture of the "breaking of the bread". After Communion and thanksgiving the liturgy of the Eucharist is brought to a close with the prayer after Communion.

Just as the Mass opened with the introductory rites so it concludes with a rite of dismissal. This is made up of the final greeting and blessing followed by the dismissal, the veneration of the altar and the procession.

The Introductory Rites

The purpose of the Introductory rite is quite simply to enable the congregation be of one mind and heart so that they are ready to listen to word of God and celebrate the holy Eucharist. Saint Benedict expresses this in his Rule by saying that in the sacred liturgy our minds should be in harmony with our voice.

Entrance Chant

When all is ready and the people have assembled together, the entrance chant begins, and the Celebrant and ministers process to the altar. The opening chant or hymn helps to introduce the assembly to the season or mystery that is being celebrated. The opening chant is the first affirmation by the assembly that they have come together to praise and worship the Lord.

"Let us come before Him singing for joy ... with songs of praise, let us hail the Lord, ... Let us come before him giving thanks ..." (from the Psalms).

Veneration of the Altar and Greeting of the People

When the Celebrant and the ministers reach the place of celebration, they make a sign of honour and reverence to the altar. The Celebrant and the ordained ministers venerate the altar with a kiss. Incense is a sign of honour and also symbolises the prayers of the people of God that ascend to heaven. The Celebrant receives the censer from the deacon or server and proceeds to walk around the altar incensing it. In front of the Cross, the Celebrant pauses and reverences the holy image with incense.

Sign of the Cross

The opening words and gesture with which the people of God begin their celebration affirm both their baptismal profession of faith in God, Father, Son and Holy Spirit and their mission to witness it before the whole world: "Go, therefore, and make disciples of all nations, baptizing them *in the name of the Father and of the Son and of the holy Spirit*" (Matthew 28:19). (cf. John 14:13-14; Acts 2:21).

All reply *Amen* which is a Hebrew word. It is meant to convey approval for what has been done or said. The expression also has the idea of a definitive affirmation "so be it for it cannot be otherwise". *Amen* occurs several times in the liturgy and always has the meaning of an affirmative assent to what has been said and accomplished.

Greeting

The community is assembled in the name of Christ Jesus, "where two or three are gathered in my name, there I am in their midst" (Matthew 18:20). This belief in the Lord's presence is shown by the greeting and acknowledged by the people's response. Any form of secular greeting, such as "good morning", is not only inappropriate but it undermines the meaning of what it is to be assembled in Christ. If there is a need for a particular word of welcome this takes place after the greeting and as part of the introduction to the Mass.

First form of greeting

The grace of our Lord Jesus Christ,
and the love of God,
and the *communion* of the Holy Spirit
be with you all.

This greeting is taken from the second letter of Saint Paul to the Corinthians, (2 Corinthians 13:13). The greetings used in the celebration of Mass are among our oldest liturgical texts and have their roots in Holy Scripture, especially the writings of St Paul. It is possible that Saint Paul was quoting words of greeting which were already in current use in the first Christian communities.

Instead of the former "fellowship of the Holy Spirit" the text now reads "communion of the Holy Spirit". The word *communion* conveys much more than is implied by fellowship. Communion is an expression of the very essence of the nature of the Church. The most fundamental fellowship is not that with one another but the communion/fellowship in the life of Christ. The greeting affirms that through the communion of the Holy Spirit we become one body, one spirit in Christ. Our fellowship in the bond of charity is the fruit of communion.

"The Church is called during her earthly pilgrimage to maintain and promote communion with the Triune God and communion among the faithful. For this purpose she possesses the word and the sacraments, particularly the Eucharist, by which she "constantly lives and grows and in which she expresses her very nature". (*Blessed John Paul II*).

Second form of greeting

Grace to you and peace from God our Father
and the Lord Jesus Christ.

This greeting is also an invocation that God will bless his people with peace. They embody the message of Saint Paul to the Philippians, an excellent preparation to our celebration, "Do not be anxious about anything, but in everything, by prayer and petition, with thanksgiving, present your requests to God. And the peace of God, which transcends all understanding, will guard your hearts and your minds in Christ Jesus." (Philippians 4:5-7)

The greeting "Grace to you and peace" is found in the oldest of new Testament writings, the first Letter of Saint Paul to the Thessalonians, which was written about the year 55. It is wonderful that these words still find a place in our celebration of the liturgy.[1]

Third form of greeting

The Lord be with you.

This the shortest and simplest of greetings is the most ancient. The phrase expresses the greatest good that a believer can wish another, namely, to be with the Lord and under Divine protection. It is also has the character of a prayer that each member of the assembly should progress ever more into the fullness of the stature of Christ.

This greeting occurs in the Old Testament, in the Book of Ruth 2:4 Boaz greets the reapers in his field with the words, "The Lord be with you". The prophet Azariah greets Asa with the words "The Lord is with you, while you are with him." (2 Chronicles 15:2).

The first Christians would, given their Jewish background, be familiar with these greetings and readily use them in their assemblies.

Instead of *The Lord be with you,* a Bishop says:

Peace be with you.

The greeting "peace be with you" was used by the risen Lord to his disciples who were gathered in the upper room. These words are a proclamation and affirmation that here in this place the mystery of the Church is made manifest.

The reply of the people to all the greetings is:

And with your spirit.

There are certain phrases in the writings of the New Testament that are of Hebrew or Aramaic origin and which have been retained even though they are not the normal way of expressing a concept in Greek or Latin. Through these expressions we maintain a dynamic link with our origins. One such expression is "And with your spirit" which Saint Paul used in his letters. To the Galatians he wrote "May the grace of our Lord Jesus Christ be with your spirit" (Galatians 6:18). With greater simplicity he greeted Timothy with the words, "the Lord be with your spirit" (2 Timothy 4:22). Similar expressions are found in Philippians 4: 23 and Philemon 25.

By the end of the third century the greeting and response was well established as is attested in a work known as "The Apostolic Tradition" written by Saint Hippolytus (170-236). The Bishop greets the newly baptized with "The Lord be with you" and receives the reply "And with your spirit".

It is not only in Greek and Latin that "And with your spirit" is found but in other ancient liturgical languages, Syriac, Georgian and Slavonic to name a few. Also in modern liturgical languages *Et cum spiritu tuo* has been translated *And with your spirit*. Italian: "E con il tuo spirito."; Spanish: "Y con tu espiritu."; French: "Et avec votre esprit."; German: "Und mit deinem Geiste.". English does not need to be an exception.

The response *And with your spirit,* is an affirmation by the people that the priest is not acting in his own name but that his ministry is from God and does not depend upon his human qualities and gifts. The response "*And with your spirit*" reminds the priest of the great responsibility he has undertaken through ordination. Saint

Paul reminded Timothy when he said, "Do not neglect the gift you have, which was given you by prophetic utterance when the council of elders laid their hands upon you." (1 Timothy 4:14).

Theodore the Bishop of Mopsuestia who was born at Antioch about 350 wrote that the word "spirit" refers to the grace of the priesthood, "In saying 'and with your spirit' they do not refer to his soul, but to the grace of the Holy Spirit by which his people believe that he is called to the priesthood" (*Baptismal Homilies*, 15, 37).

The fifth century Bishop Narsi of Nisibis in Syria gives this explanation, "The people answer the priest devoutly saying: 'With you, O priest, and with that priestly spirit of yours.' They call 'spirit' not that soul which is in the priest, but the spirit which the priest has received by the laying on of hands. By the laying on of hands the priest receives the power of the Spirit so that he may be able to perform the divine mysteries. That grace the people call the spirit of the priest and they pray that he may attain peace with it and it with him" (*Exposition of the Mysteries*, Homily 17 A).

The great Patriarch of Constantinople and Doctor of the Church Saint John Chrysostom explained to his congregation that "spirit" in the reply which they give to the bishop shows that the bishop celebrates the holy sacrifice, not in his own name, but in the power of the Holy Spirit.

"If there was no Holy Spirit there would be no shepherds or teachers in the Church, for these also come through the Spirit. As St Paul says: 'In which flock the Holy Spirit has established you shepherds and bishops'. Do you not see how this also comes about through the Spirit? For if the Holy Spirit was not in this father and teacher when just now he went up into the sanctuary and gave all of you the peace, you would not all have answered: 'And with your Spirit.'".

"For this reason, you give this reply not only when he goes up into the sanctuary and when he addresses you and when he prays for you, but when he stands at the sacred table and when he begins to offer the awe-inspiring sacrifice... By this reply, 'And with your spirit' you are also reminded that the right offering of the gifts is not a work of human nature, but that the mystic sacrifice is brought about by the grace of the Holy Spirit and his hovering over all. For he who is there is a man, it is God who works though him. Do not attend to the nature of the one you see, but understand the grace which is invisible. Nothing human takes place in this sacred sanctuary. If the spirit was not present there would be no Church assisting, but if the Church stands round it is clear that the Spirit is present."

The Penitential Act

After greeting the people, the Priest invites the faithful to participate in a Penitential Act. This is an acknowledgement of our unworthiness so that our hearts and minds may be made ready to celebrate the sacred mysteries. The Penitential Act is concluded by the priest imploring the Lord's pardon and forgiveness.

The Penitential Act reminds us that we have come into the presence of the Lord, we are "in his holy temple, the place where God dwells".

Moses was told to remove his sandals in God's presence for he was standing on holy ground. All who ministered in the Temple purified themselves before entering upon their ministry.

We see in many parts of holy Scripture especially in the writings of the prophets who were privileged in their experience of God, that there is always an intense awareness of unworthiness in the presence of the All Holy. For this reason the prophet Isaiah asked that his lips might be purified (Isaiah 6:5-7).

The Penitential Act has its roots in a tradition that can be traced to the earliest times. An ancient Church document known as the *Didache* and believed to have been written between the year 90 and 100 states that "On the Lord's day gather together, break bread and give thanks after confessing your transgressions so that your sacrifice may be pure. Let no one who has a quarrel with his neighbour join you until he is reconciled, lest your sacrifice be defiled. For this is that which was proclaimed by the Lord, 'In every place and time let there be offered to Me a clean Sacrifice'".

Call to repentance

Brethren (brothers and sisters),
let us acknowledge our sins,
and so prepare ourselves
to celebrate the sacred mysteries.

To acknowledge our sin is also a sign of trust in the mercy of God. Saint Cyprian expresses this in his commentary on the Lord's Prayer:

"When the publican prayed with the Pharisee in the temple he did not lift up his eyes boldly to heaven, nor proudly raise his hands; but *beating his breast*, and testifying to the sins shut up within, he implored the help of the divine mercy. This man deserved to be sanctified, since he placed the hope of salvation not in the confidence of his innocence, because there is none who is innocent; but confessing his sinfulness he humbly prayed, and He who pardons the humble heard the petitioner".

We have come into the presence of the Lord giving thanks and by acknowledging our sin we also give thanks for his gracious love and mercy because we know that the Lord is merciful and that He will grant us his gift of pardon and peace.

> I confess to almighty God
> and to you, my brothers and sisters,
> that I have greatly sinned,
> in my thoughts and in my words,
> in what I have done and in what I have failed to do,
> *(and, striking their breast, they say)*
> through my fault, through my fault,
> through my most grievous fault;

In Holy Scripture striking one's breast is a way of showing profound sorrow for having offended God. This action was also adopted by Christians so much so that Saint Augustine said that, "No sooner have you heard the word 'Confiteor' than you strike your breast. What does this mean except that you wish to bring to light what is concealed in the breast, and by this act to cleanse your hidden sins?"

Body language is important as a form of communication which also enhances and explains verbal communication. Since signs and symbols are such an integral part of the Liturgy, body language, such as striking the breast, has a place in our celebrations. Other examples of liturgical body language are bowing the head and the profound bow. The act of standing, sitting and kneeling in a common movement says something about the assembly. Good posture is encouraged even in secular society as an aid to good health. A healthy liturgical assembly needs to be attentive to posture. The celebrant too needs to pay attention to his actions and gestures.

The repetition of "through my fault" is meant to convey the sincerity of the words expressing repentance. When we make an apology we admit our mistake and express our regret by more than just two or three words.

> therefore I ask blessed Mary ever-Virgin,
> all the Angels and Saints,
> and you, my brothers and sisters,
> to pray for me to the Lord our God.

We ask the Blessed Virgin Mary, the Angels, and the Saints to pray for us because we do not wish to stand alone before the judgement seat of God. We also ask for the help and support of our brothers and sisters. Praying for others is also a work of charity and "charity covers a multitude of sins".

"Therefore confess your sins to each other and pray for each other so that you may be healed. The prayer of a righteous man is powerful and effective". (James 5:16)

The absolution

After each of the various forms of the Penitential Act the celebrant invokes the mercy of God so that with our sins forgiven we may be admitted to the heavenly kingdom.

May almighty God have mercy on us, forgive us our sins, and bring us to everlasting life. Amen.

Lord, have mercy

With the words "Lord have mercy" the faithful acclaim the Lord and implore His mercy. When it is used in the Penitential Act it is an appeal for the mercy of God.

When the *Lord, have mercy* was first introduced into the liturgy it was in the form of a litany. The word litany comes from the Greek and means to make an appeal with fervour and humility.

As part of the Penitential Act it is a call for God's mercy. When it is sung or said after the Penitential Act it has the character of praising God for his mercy.

Without prejudice to the English translation, to keep the Greek form *Kyrie eleison* would be a link for us to the life of the early Church. It was originally from the Eastern liturgies but was added to the Roman rite at the end of the 4th century by Pope Gelasius I (492-496). It remained unchanged in the liturgy for 1500 years, it is still used by our Greek brothers and sisters.

The hymn 'Glory to God in the Highest'

The 'Glory to God in the highest' is an ancient Greek hymn with which the Church, gathered in the Holy Spirit, glorifies and praises God. The opening words of the hymn are taken from the Gospel of Saint Luke (2:13-14): "And suddenly there was with the angel a multitude of the heavenly host praising God and saying, "Glory to God in the highest, and on earth peace to people of good will.".". The words of the Angels are an announcement, a declaration that God is glorified and we are reconciled to Him through the mystery of the Incarnation, the birth of our Saviour in Bethlehem.

This joyful hymn calls upon the faithful to celebrate the glory of God, Father, Son, and Holy Spirit: "You alone are the Most High, Jesus Christ, with the Holy Spirit, in the glory of God the Father."

The first part of the "Gloria" is made up of a series of acclamations glorifying God the Father with a crescendo of praise reaching its climax in the words "we give you thanks for your great glory".

Glory to God in the highest,
and on earth peace to people of good will.
We praise you,

we bless you,
we adore you,
we glorify you,
we give you thanks for your great glory,
Lord God, heavenly King,
O God, almighty Father.

The second part of the hymn is directed to our Lord Jesus Christ with phrases that echo the Gospel of Saint John. The call for mercy and to receive our prayer are a response to the Lord's words, "Whatever you ask in my name, I will do it, that the Father may be glorified in the Son; if you ask anything in my name, I will do it". (John 14:13-14).

Lord Jesus Christ, Only Begotten Son,   (John 1:14)
Lord God, Lamb of God, Son of the Father,
you take away the sins of the world,   (John 1:29)
have mercy on us;
you take away the sins of the world,
receive our prayer;
you are seated at the right hand of the Father,
have mercy on us.

"seek the things that are above, where Christ is, seated at the right hand of God". (Colossians 3:1).

The third part of the hymn praises the Holy Trinity and recalls Saint Paul's words to the Philippians let "every tongue confess that Jesus Christ is Lord, to the glory of God the Father.

> For you alone are the Holy One,
> you alone are the Lord,
> you alone are the Most High,
> Jesus Christ,
> with the Holy Spirit,
> in the glory of God the Father. Amen.

"For you alone are holy". (Revelation 15:4).

"Let them know that you alone, you whose name is the Lord, are the Most High over all the earth". (Psalms 83:19).

"This angelic song has been recognized from the earliest days as music proceeding from God, indeed, as an invitation to join in the singing with hearts filled with joy at the fact that we are loved by God. Saint Augustine says that singing is a mark of one who loves. Thus, down the centuries, the angels' song has again and again become a song of love and joy, a song of those who love". (*Pope Benedict XVI*).

The Collect

These words, *Let us pray*, remind us that "Our prayer is public and common; and when we pray, we pray not for one, but for the whole people, because we the whole people are one. The God of peace and the Teacher of concord, who taught unity, willed that one should thus pray for all, even as He Himself bore us all in one". (*St Cyprian*).

The prayer is addressed to the Father and makes a petition related to the season, feast or particular celebration. The collect ends with the following formula which expresses the Lord's command to pray to the Father in his name:

through Christ our Lord, who lives and reigns with you (the Father) in the unity of the Holy Spirit, God for ever and ever. Amen.

The Liturgy of the Word

The Liturgy of the Word opens with the readings from Sacred Scripture and the chants occurring between them. In the readings God speaks to his people. The mystery of redemption and salvation is revealed and spiritual nourishment given. Christ the Lord is present through his word in the midst of the faithful. By silence and by singing, the people make this divine word their own. The Homily explains the Word and the Profession of Faith affirms it. In conclusion the people pour out their petitions by means of the Prayer of the Faithful for the needs of the whole Church and for the salvation of the whole world.

The Readings

In the readings, the table of God's word is spread before the faithful, and the treasures of the Bible are opened to them. The image of the two tables, the Word of God and the Eucharist, is found in the teaching of the great Fathers of the Church. St Augustine declared, "from the table of the Lord we receive the bread of life... And from the table of Sunday readings we are nourished with the doctrine of the Lord". (*Commentary on Psalm 127*:10)

This teaching is also found for example in the great classic of the Middle Ages *The Imitation of Christ* "there are two tables placed among the treasures of the Church. One is the table of the holy altar on which rests a consecrated bread, the precious body of Jesus Christ. The other is the table of the divine Law. This contains the holy doctrine of the true faith, which lifts the veil of the sanctuary and leads us securely into the very Holy of holies". (Book 4, ch. 11).

"Do you want to know what the Bible is? If you want to have some idea look at the Tabernacle. What do you see? The Word of God Incarnate under the species of bread and wine as food for our souls. Look now at the Bible; what do you see? The Divine Word, the wisdom of the Father, who speaks to us therein until the end of time. There, He is truly present, a real presence. The Lord gives himself to us under two aspects; he gives us himself to teach us in the Holy Scriptures; he gives us himself to nourish us in the Eucharist. The two mysteries are complementary; the Church does not offer the Holy Sacrifice without the accompaniment of readings drawn from the Old and the New Testament; these readings are designed to indicate this double presence: the real substantial presence in the divine Host, and the presence no less real in the Scriptures". (Abbot Prosper Guéranger, *Retreat Notes*, 1863).

The Word of the Lord (1 Peter 1:25)

After each reading the assembled people by their acclamation "Thanks be to God" show that they have heard and welcomed the Word of God in faith and with gratitude. (Romans 6:17; 2 Corinthians 9:15).

Responsorial Psalm

The psalm which follows the First Reading is a prayerful meditation on the word of God. It also takes up the acclamation "Thanks be to God" because it is a more solemn assent to the Reading. It often happens that the psalm itself takes on a deeper meaning in the light of the passage from Scripture which has just been read.

When the psalm cannot be sung, it should be read slowly and attention given to its poetical character and rhythm.

In a sung Mass, an appropriate Gradual from the repertoire of Gregorian Chants given in the *Graduale Roman* may be used.

The Gospel Acclamation Alleluia

Saint Augustine in his Commentary on the Psalms wrote "We have a custom of singing Alleluia at a certain time in our solemnities, after an old tradition of the Church: in this word is signified the praise of God".

After the reading that immediately precedes the Gospel, the Alleluia and its verse are sung.

Through this acclamation the faithful welcome and greet the Lord who is about to speak to them in the Gospel.

The Gospel

The ceremonial and marks of honour that accompany the proclamation of the Gospel show that this is the most sacred moment of the Liturgy of the Word. The one who is to proclaim the Gospel makes a special preparation. The deacon receives a Blessing:

May the Lord be in your heart and on your lips
that you may proclaim his Gospel worthily and well,
in the name of the Father and of the Son
and of the Holy Spirit.

In the absence of a Deacon the Priest prepares himself by bowing before the altar and saying quietly, "Cleanse my heart and my lips, almighty God, that I may worthily proclaim your holy Gospel".

In a solemn celebration, the Gospel book is carried in procession to the place of its proclamation accompanied by candles and incense. Such marks of reverence help to prepare the minds and hearts of all present as they stand to listen to the holy reading.

"When the Gospel is to be read at Mass, stand up to show that you are ready and equipped to walk on the way that the Gospel commands. To stir your devotion, you can say as you do so, 'Jesus Christ was made obedient unto death, even the death of the cross.'" (*St Francis de Sales*).

Glory to you, O Lord

The meaning of these words is most aptly expressed by Saint Augustine, "Let us therefore hear the Gospel just as if we were listening to the Lord himself present: nor let us say, 'O happy they who were able to see him!' Because there were many of the them who saw, and also killed him; and there are many among us who has not seen him, and yet have believed. For the precious truth that sounded forth from the mouth of our Lord was both written for our sake, and preserved for our sake, and recited for our sake, and will be recited even until the end of the world".

While announcing the passage of the Gospel to be read the deacon or priest makes the Sign of the Cross on the book and on his forehead, lips, and breast, which everyone else does as well. This outward gesture expresses the desire that the words of the Holy Gospel should be in our mind, in our mouth, and in our heart.

At the end of the proclamation of the Gospel, the Deacon, or the Priest, acclaims:

The Gospel of the Lord, and all reply:
Praise to you, Lord Jesus Christ.

These words declare that we believe that through the power of the Holy Spirit, the Lord is present to us in the proclamation of the Gospel. The kissing of the book is not only a sign of reverence but an acknowledgement of the presence of the Holy Spirit. The proclamation of the Gospel is always a call to conversion, "repent and believe in the Gospel" and so the kissing of the book is accompanied by the words:

Through the words of the Gospel may our sins be wiped away.

The Homily

The good news of the Gospel was proclaimed and preached before it was written down. The homily is the continuation of this ancient tradition. We are told in the Book of the Acts of the Apostles that the Christian community came together to listen to the teaching of the apostles and break bread.

It is in the homily that the preacher breaks the bread of the Word of God for the nourishment of the faith of the Christian community. The one who gives the homily teaches in the name of the Church and serves the living tradition of the Church. This is a great responsibility.

"The homily is a means of bringing the scriptural message to life in a way that helps the faithful to realize that God's word is present and at work in their everyday lives. It should lead to an understanding of the mystery being celebrated, serve as a summons to mission, and prepare the assembly for the profession of faith, the universal prayer and the Eucharistic liturgy". (*Pope Benedict XVI*).

The Creed: Profession of Faith

At the end of the Homily, the Profession of Faith, (when prescribed), is either sung or said. The Creed was formulated at the Council of Nicaea in 325 and revised at the Council of Constantinople in 385 and so is called the Nicene Constantinopolitan Creed. The Creed is a developed form of the questions that were put to the candidate for baptism.

The Creed always reminds us of our baptism. It originally was part of the right of Christian initiation. The use of the Creed at Mass began in the East where it was seen as a fitting preparation leading to the celebration of the sacred mysteries. The Creed was introduced into the Mass in Rome in the 11th century as an acclamation of the Word of God through which our faith has been given to us.

As Pope Benedict XVI pointed out, "The Creed is not a collection of propositions; it is not a theory. It is anchored in the event of Baptism – a genuine encounter between God and man. In the mystery of Baptism, God stoops to meet us; He comes close to us and in turn brings us closer to one another".

The Creed is an expression of personal adherence to the faith of the Church and so begins with the declaration "I believe".

I believe in one God,
the Father almighty,
maker of heaven and earth,
of all things visible and invisible.

Just as the Book of Genesis begins with God creating heaven and earth, so our profession of faith begins with the Father the creator of heaven and earth.

Thus says the Lord, your Redeemer: "I am the Lord, who made all things, who stretched out the heavens alone, who spread out the earth". (Isaiah 44:24).

I believe in one Lord Jesus Christ,
the Only Begotten Son of God,
born of the Father before all ages.
God from God, Light from Light,
true God from true God,
begotten, not made, consubstantial with the Father;
through him all things were made.

"God is light, and in him is no darkness at all". (1 John 1:5).

Jesus Christ "is the image of the invisible God, the first-born of all creation; for in him all things were created, in heaven and on earth, visible and invisible". (Colossians 1:15-16).

Consubstantial with the Father

Consubstantial is a Christian word from an original Greek term decided by the Fathers of the Council of Nicea to be apt to express our Catholic faith. The Church has her own theological vocabulary which cannot be discarded.

"The Incarnation of God's Son reveals that God is the eternal Father and that the Son is consubstantial with the Father, which means that, in the Father and with the Father the Son is one and the same God". (CCC 262).

"He was in the beginning with God; all things were made through him, and without him was not anything made that was made". (John 1:2-3). "I and the Father are one". (John 10:30).

> For us men and for our salvation
> he came down from heaven,
> and by the Holy Spirit was incarnate
> of the Virgin Mary,
> and became man.

This article of faith finds expression in the teaching of Saint John's Gospel that "For God so loved the world that He gave His only Son, that whoever believe in Him should not perish but have eternal life. For God sent the Son into the world, not to condemn the world, but that the world might be saved through Him" (John 3:16-17). The profound bow at the words "and became man" is a sign of our faith in the mystery of the Incarnation.

> For our sake he was crucified under Pontius Pilate,
> he suffered death and was buried,

and rose again on the third day
in accordance with the Scriptures.

"From that time Jesus began to show his disciples that
he must go to Jerusalem and suffer many things from the
elders and chief priests and scribes, and be killed, and on
the third day be raised". (Matthew 16:21).

He ascended into heaven
and is seated at the right hand of the Father.
He will come again in glory
to judge the living and the dead
and his kingdom will have no end.

Jesus said, "I am ascending to my Father and your
Father, to my God and your God". (John 20:17). "So then
the Lord Jesus, after he had spoken to them, was taken up
into heaven, and sat down at the right hand of
God".(Mark 16:19).

I believe in the Holy Spirit, the Lord, the giver of life,
who proceeds from the Father and the Son,
who with the Father and the Son
is adored and glorified,
who has spoken through the prophets.

"The Spirit gives life". (2 Corinthians 3:6).
"For no prophecy ever came through human will; but
rather human beings moved by the holy Spirit spoke
under the influence of God". (2 Peter 1:21).

"The Holy Spirit proceeds from the Father as the first principle and, by the eternal gift of this to the Son, from the communion of both the Father and the Son". (*St Augustine*).

"But when the Counsellor comes, whom I shall send to you from the Father, even the Spirit of truth, who proceeds from the Father, he will bear witness to me". (John 15:26).

I believe in one, holy, catholic and apostolic Church.
I confess one Baptism for the forgiveness of sins
and I look forward to the resurrection of the dead
and the life of the world to come. Amen.

"One Lord, one faith, one baptism". (Ephesians 4:5).

"For God so loved the world that he gave his only Son, that whoever believes in him should not perish but have eternal life". (John 3:16).

The Apostles' Creed

Instead of the Niceno-Constantinopolitan Creed, especially during Lent and Easter Time, the baptismal Symbol of the Roman Church, known as the Apostles' Creed, may be used.

"The Church, for her part, has given us a tiny *Summa* (a statement of faith) in which everything essential is expressed. It is the so-called 'Apostles' Creed', which is usually divided into twelve articles, corresponding to the number of the twelve Apostles. It speaks of God, the creator and source of all that is, of Christ and His work of salvation, and it culminates in the resurrection of the dead and life everlasting." (*Pope Benedict XVI*).

I believe in God, the Father almighty,
Creator of heaven and earth,
and in Jesus Christ, his only Son, our Lord,
(At the words that follow, up to and including the Virgin Mary, all bow.)
who was conceived by the Holy Spirit,
born of the Virgin Mary,
suffered under Pontius Pilate,
was crucified, died and was buried;
he descended into hell;

"By the expression 'He descended into hell', the Apostles' Creed confesses that Jesus did really die and through his death for us conquered death and the devil 'who has the power of death'" (CCC 636).

on the third day he rose again from the dead;
he ascended into heaven,
and is seated at the right hand of God
the Father almighty;
from there he will come to judge the living and the dead.

"Faith in the Resurrection has as its object an event which as historically attested to by the disciples, who really encountered the Risen One. At the same time, this event is mysteriously transcendent insofar as it is the entry of Christ's humanity into the glory of God". (CCC 656).

> I believe in the Holy Spirit,
> the holy catholic Church,
> the communion of saints,
> the forgiveness of sins,
> the resurrection of the body,
> and life everlasting. Amen.

"As Christians, we say: 'I believe in God the Father, the Creator of heaven and earth' - I believe in the Creator Spirit. We believe that at the beginning of everything is the eternal Word, with Reason and not Unreason. With this faith we have no reason to hide, no fear of ending up in a dead end. We rejoice that we can know God! And we try to help others see the reasonableness of faith, as Saint Peter in his First Letter explicitly urged the Christians of his time to do, and with them, ourselves as well! (cf. 3:15)". (*Pope Benedict XVI*).

The Universal Prayer, the Prayer of the Faithful or Bidding Prayers

The General intercessions or the Prayer of the Faithful are of ancient origin. Saint Paul suggested intentions for prayer when he wrote to Timothy that there should be "prayers, petitions, intercessions and thanksgiving for all: for rulers and all in authority, so that we may be able to live quiet and peaceful lives in the full practice of religion and of morality" (1 Timothy 2:1-4).

Saint Justin (c.155) wrote that "on the Lord's day, after the reading of Scripture and the homily, all stand and offer the prayers" (*First Apology*, 67).

These prayers are called the Prayer of the Faithful because they were begun after the departure of the Catechumens and those who were not yet baptised. The Baptised Faithful exercise their priestly function by interceding for the needs of all of humanity. The prayer which concludes the Intercessions is also marks the end of the Liturgy of the Word.

The Liturgy of the Eucharist

The presentation of the gifts

The Liturgy of the Eucharist begins with the preparation of the gifts. This rite should not be seen as an "interval" between the liturgy of the word and the liturgy of the Eucharist. "This humble and simple gesture is very significant: in the bread and wine that we bring to the altar, all creation is taken up by Christ the Redeemer to be transformed and presented to the Father. In this way we also bring to the altar all the pain and suffering of the world, in the certainty that everything has value in God's eyes. God invites us to participate in bringing to fulfilment his handiwork, and in so doing, gives human labour its authentic meaning, since, through the celebration of the Eucharist, it is united to the redemptive sacrifice of Christ". (*Pope Benedict XVI*).

The corporal, purificator, chalice, pall, and the Missal are placed on the altar. The faithful express their participation by making an offering and bringing forward bread and wine for the celebration of the Eucharist.

"Blessed are you, Lord, God of all creation..."

(cf. 1 Chronicles 29:10; Psalms 72:18-19; 119:10; Luke 1:68). The bread and wine are a symbol of the earth's produce and our life and work. They come to us through the goodness of God our Father from whom every good gift comes. These humble gifts, the fruit of the earth and work of human hands, will become for us the bread of life and our spiritual drink.

"God who is over all be blessed forever". (Romans 9:5).

The Deacon, or the Priest, pours wine and a little water into the chalice, saying quietly:

By the mystery of this water and wine
may we come to share in the divinity of Christ
who humbled himself to share in our humanity.

This mingling of a little water with the wine was the normal practice at the time of our Lord. The words which accompany this act are taken from the Collect for the Mass of Christmas Day. This prayer praises God for the great mystery of the Incarnation whereby through his sharing in our human nature, Christ Jesus gave us a share in his divine nature.

In the year 253 Saint Cyprian wrote that the practice of mingling water with wine was "according to the tradition of the Lord". For the holy bishop the drop of water was a sign that the Church was participating in the sacrifice of Christ. The wine represents Christ our Lord and the water the people whom he redeemed through his precious blood and washed clean in the waters of baptism.

The prayer of a "humble spirit and contrite heart" is acceptable to God (Psalm 51:19) and so the priest prays that through our humble prayer our sacrifice may be pleasing to the Lord our God. This prayer is further developed as the priest washes his hands and asks that the Lord will wash away his iniquity and cleanse him from sin.

"But with contrite heart and humble spirit let us be received ... So let our sacrifice be in your presence today and find favour before you" (Daniel 3:39-40).

Pray, brethren (brothers and sisters),
that my sacrifice and yours may be acceptable to God,
the almighty Father.

When the priest asks the people to pray that the sacrifice may be acceptable he is affirming that we do not presume on God's goodness and mercy. We trust in God, we know that He is faithful and that He will receive the sacrifice of a humbled and contrite heart. Nevertheless, we approach the sacred mysteries with humility and trust.

The distinction "my sacrifice and yours" is because the priest acts in the person of Christ, not in his own name, and at the same time the people exercise their priesthood, which is different but complementary.

May the Lord accept the sacrifice at your hands
for the praise and glory of his name,
for our good and the good of all his holy Church.

Holy is the most ancient adjective describing the Church.

The Prayer over the Offerings

Just as the Collect prayer closes the Introductory rites, so the Prayer over the Gifts concludes the rite of preparation. In ancient times this prayer was the only formulary used at the presentation of the gifts. These prayers are not so complex as the Collect prayers and usually acknowledge the gifts on the altar and the good will of those who have brought them knowing that they will become the pledge of eternal salvation.

The Eucharistic Prayers

"The Eucharistic Prayer is 'the centre and summit of the entire celebration'. The different Eucharistic Prayers contained in the Missal have been handed down to us by the Church's living Tradition and are noteworthy for their inexhaustible theological and spiritual richness". (*Pope Benedict XVI*).

Lift up your hearts.
We lift them up to the Lord.

In chapter 3 of the Book of Lamentations which speaks of hope for God's people we read "Let us lift up our hearts and our hands to God in heaven". The raising of hearts and hands indicates the total self giving to prayer without distraction.

This is affirmed by Saint Cyprian who tells us that "when we stand praying, we ought to be watchful and earnest with our whole heart, intent on our prayers. Let all carnal and worldly thoughts pass away, nor let the soul at that time think on anything but the object only of its prayer." For this reason also the priest, by way of preface before his prayer, prepares the minds of the brethren by saying, "Lift up your hearts," that so upon the people's response, "We lift them up unto the Lord," he may be reminded that he himself ought to think of nothing but the Lord.

Let us give thanks to the Lord our God.
It is right and just.

"Eucharist" comes from the Greek word for thanks. Let us give thanks at this moment of the liturgy takes on a special significance. The call to give thanks in the Preface is a pre-intonation of making the offering of the Eucharist. The assent of the people is taken up by the celebrant and becomes the opening words of the Eucharistic Prayer.

Every Preface begins in the same way:

It is truly right and just.

The Preface is an integral part of the Eucharistic Prayer. Its character is that of a hymn of praise. The Father is given thanks for the gifts of creation and His providential care. In the words of Saint Paul, "always and for everything giving thanks in the name of our Lord Jesus Christ". The wonders that God has done for us through His Son, Jesus Christ our Lord call for a "chorus of exultant praise". As the Preface draws to a close we are called upon to unite our voices with the Angels and the whole heavenly host so that heaven and earth sing the praises of God.

Holy, Holy, Holy Lord God of hosts.
Heaven and earth are full of your glory.
Hosanna in the highest.
Blessed is he who comes in the name of the Lord.
Hosanna in the highest.

This hymn to the infinite holiness of God is found in the Eucharistic Prayers of both the Western and Eastern Church since the fourth century.

Both parts of this solemn acclamation are drawn from Scripture. "I saw the Lord, high and exalted, seated on a throne ... and above him were seraphim ... and they were calling to one another: "Holy, holy, holy is the Lord of hosts; the whole earth is full of his glory". (Isaiah 6:1-5. See also Revelation 4:2-8).

As Jesus entered Jerusalem "the crowds that went before him and that followed him were shouting, "Hosanna to the Son of David! Blessed is he who comes in the name of the Lord! Hosanna in the highest!" (Matthew 21: 9).

Eucharistic Prayer I
(The Roman Canon)

"After the Sanctus, think with all humility and reverence of the great blessing of the death and passion of our Saviour; ask him to bring it to all the world, especially to the children of the Church and to those who are close to us. Ask him that it may be for the glory and happiness of the saints in heaven, and a solace for the souls in Purgatory". (*St Francis de Sales*).

To you, therefore, most merciful Father,
we make humble prayer and petition
through Jesus Christ, your Son, our Lord:

"The initial letter of the first Prayer of the Canon is T which by its very shape, represents a Cross. No other sign could better be placed as a heading to this Great Prayer, in the course of which the Sacrifice of Calvary is renewed". (*Abbot Prosper Guéranger*).

that you accept
and bless these gifts, these offerings,
these holy and unblemished sacrifices,
which we offer you firstly
for your holy catholic Church.

Be pleased to grant her peace,
to guard, unite and govern her
throughout the whole world,
together with your servant N. our Pope
and N. our Bishop,
and all those who, holding to the truth,
hand on the catholic and apostolic faith.

The Eucharistic Prayer developed its form quite early as can be seen in this description given by Saint Cyril of Jerusalem (313-386), "We beg God to grant peace to all the Churches, to give harmony to the whole world, to bless our rulers, our soldiers and our companions, to aid the sick and afflicted, and in general to assist all those who stand in need; we all pray for all these intentions and we offer this victim for them ... and last of all for our deceased holy forefathers and bishops and for all those who have lived among us. For we have a deep conviction that great help will be afforded those souls for whom prayers are offered while this holy and awesome victim is present".

Commemoration of the Living

Remember, Lord, your servants N. and N.
and all gathered here,
whose faith and devotion are known to you.
For them, we offer you this sacrifice of praise
or they offer it for themselves

and all who are dear to them,
for the redemption of their souls,
in hope of health and well-being,
and paying their homage to you,
the eternal God, living and true.

"Offer to God the sacrifice of praise: and pay thy vows
to the most High". (Psalms 50:14).
"My vows to the Lord I will fulfill before all his
people" (Psalms 116:14-18)

In communion with those whose memory we venerate,
especially the glorious ever-Virgin Mary,
Mother of our God and Lord, Jesus Christ,
† and blessed Joseph, her Spouse,
your blessed Apostles and Martyrs,
Peter and Paul, Andrew,
(James, John,
Thomas, James, Philip,
Bartholomew, Matthew,
Simon and Jude:
Linus, Cletus, Clement, Sixtus,
Cornelius, Cyprian,
Lawrence, Chrysogonus,
John and Paul,
Cosmas and Damian)
and all your Saints:
we ask that through their merits and prayers,

in all things we may be defended
by your protecting help.

"The bread which we break, is it not a communion in the body of Christ? Because there is one bread, we who are many are one body, for we all partake of the one bread". (1 Corinthians 10:16-17).

Therefore, Lord, we pray:
graciously accept this oblation of our service,
that of your whole family;
order our days in your peace,
and command that we be delivered
from eternal damnation
and counted among the flock of those you have chosen.

Be pleased, O God, we pray,
to bless, acknowledge,
and approve this offering in every respect;
make it spiritual and acceptable,
so that it may become for us
the Body and Blood of your most beloved Son,
our Lord Jesus Christ.

"Offering spiritual sacrifices acceptable to God through Jesus Christ". (1 Peter 2:5).

"I urge you therefore, brothers, by the mercies of God, to offer your bodies as a living sacrifice, holy and pleasing to God, your spiritual worship". (Romans 12:1).

On the day before he was to suffer,
he took bread in his holy and venerable hands,
and with eyes raised to heaven
to you, O God, his almighty Father,
giving you thanks he said the blessing,
broke the bread
and gave it to his disciples, saying:
TAKE THIS, ALL OF YOU, AND EAT OF IT,
FOR THIS IS MY BODY,
WHICH WILL BE GIVEN UP FOR YOU.

"These words that Jesus spoke at the Last Supper are repeated every time that the Eucharistic Sacrifice is renewed. They lead us in spirit to the Upper Room, they make us relive the spiritual atmosphere of that night when, celebrating Easter with his followers, the Lord mystically anticipated the sacrifice that was to be consummated the following day on the Cross. The Institution of the Eucharist thus appears to us as an anticipation and acceptance, on Jesus' part, of his death. St Ephrem the Syrian writes on this topic: during the Supper Jesus sacrificed himself; on the Cross he was sacrificed by others". (*Pope Benedict XVI*).

In a similar way, when supper was ended,
he took this precious chalice
in his holy and venerable hands,
and once more giving you thanks, he said the blessing

and gave the chalice to his disciples, saying:
TAKE THIS, ALL OF YOU, AND DRINK FROM IT,
FOR THIS IS THE CHALICE OF MY BLOOD,
THE BLOOD OF THE NEW
AND ETERNAL COVENANT,
WHICH WILL BE POURED OUT FOR YOU
AND FOR MANY
FOR THE FORGIVENESS OF SINS.
DO THIS IN MEMORY OF ME.

"For this is my blood of the covenant, which is poured out for many for the forgiveness of sins". (Matt 26:28).

"He bore the sins of many, and interceded for the transgressors". (Isaiah 53:12).

"With these words Jesus presents himself as the true and definitive sacrifice, in which was fulfilled the expiation of sins which, in the Old Testament rites, was never fully completed. Our Lord Jesus Christ says that his Blood 'is poured out for many' with a comprehensible reference to the songs of the Servant of God that are found in the Book of Isaiah. With the addition 'blood of the Covenant' Jesus also makes clear that through his death the prophesy of the new Covenant is fulfilled, based on the fidelity and infinite love of the Son made man. An alliance that, therefore, is stronger than all humanity's sins. It was during the Last Supper that he made this new Covenant with his disciples and humanity, with his own

Blood, which became the 'Blood of the New Covenant'. (*Pope Benedict XVI*).

The mystery of faith

"Hold the mystery of the faith with a clear conscience". (1Timothy 3:9).

We proclaim your Death, O Lord,
and profess your Resurrection
until you come again.

When we eat this Bread and drink this Cup,
we proclaim your Death, O Lord,
until you come again.

"For as often as you eat this bread and drink the cup, you proclaim the death of the Lord until he comes" (1 Corinthians 11:26).

Save us, Saviour of the world,
for by your Cross and Resurrection
you have set us free.

"We know that this is truly the saviour of the world" (John 4:42)

The Eucharist is the mystery of a covenant. "The prayers and rites of the Eucharistic sacrifice revive the whole history of salvation continuously before the eyes of our soul, in the course of the liturgical cycle and make us

enter its significance ever more deeply" (*St Teresa
Benedicta of the Cross*).

Therefore, O Lord,
as we celebrate the memorial of the blessed Passion,
the Resurrection from the dead,
and the glorious Ascension into heaven
of Christ, your Son, our Lord,
we, your servants and your holy people,
offer to your glorious majesty
from the gifts that you have given us,
this pure victim,
this holy victim,
this spotless victim,
the holy Bread of eternal life
and the Chalice of everlasting salvation.

"I am the bread of life" (John 6:35-48)
"The chalice of salvation I will raise; I will call on the
name of the Lord" (Psalms 116:13)

Be pleased to look upon these offerings
with a serene and kindly countenance,
and to accept them,
as once you were pleased to accept
the gifts of your servant Abel the just,
the sacrifice of Abraham, our father in faith,
and the offering of your high priest Melchizedek,
a holy sacrifice, a spotless victim.

The three great sacrifices of the Old Testament are mentioned: Abel "who offered the firstlings of his flock" (Genesis 4:4). Abraham whose obedience to God knew no limit even to offering up his son (Genesis 22:1-14) and the priest-king Melchisedech who offered "bread and wine" (Gen 14, 18-20).

In humble prayer we ask you, almighty God:
command that these gifts be borne
by the hands of your holy Angel
to your altar on high
in the sight of your divine majesty,
so that all of us who through this participation
at the altar receive
the most holy Body and Blood of your Son,
may be filled with every grace and heavenly blessing.

"Look at Israel according to the flesh; are not those who eat the sacrifices participants in the altar?" (1 Corinthians 10:18).

Remember also, Lord, your servants N. and N.,
who have gone before us with the sign of faith
and rest in the sleep of peace.
Grant them, O Lord, we pray,
and all who sleep in Christ,
a place of refreshment, light and peace.

To us, also, your servants, who, though sinners,
hope in your abundant mercies,
graciously grant some share
and fellowship with your holy Apostles and Martyrs:
with John the Baptist, Stephen,
Matthias, Barnabas,
(Ignatius, Alexander, Marcellinus, Peter,
Felicity, Perpetua, Agatha, Lucy,
Agnes, Cecilia, Anastasia)
and all your Saints:
admit us, we beseech you,
into their company,
not weighing our merits,
but granting us your pardon,
through Christ our Lord.

Through whom
you continue to make all these good things, O Lord;
you sanctify them, fill them with life,
bless them, and bestow them upon us.

Through him, and with him, and in him,
O God, almighty Father,
in the unity of the Holy Spirit,
all glory and honour is yours,
for ever and ever. Amen.

Eucharistic Prayer II

The second Eucharistic prayer is based on that composed by the Roman priest and martyr Saint Hippolytus around 215 and is the earliest Eucharistic prayer that has come down to us.

It is truly right and just, our duty and our salvation,
always and everywhere to give you thanks, Father most holy,
through your beloved Son, Jesus Christ,
your Word through whom you made all things,
whom you sent as our Saviour and Redeemer,
incarnate by the Holy Spirit and born of the Virgin.
(cf. the Creed)
Fulfilling your will and gaining for you a holy people,
he stretched out his hands as he endured his Passion,
so as to break the bonds of death and manifest the resurrection.
And so, with the Angels and all the Saints
we declare your glory,
as with one voice we acclaim:
Holy, Holy, Holy Lord God of hosts....

"In the beginning was the Word ... Through him all things were made". (John 1: 1-3).

"I have stretched out My hands all day long to a rebellious people". (Isaiah 65:2).

You are indeed Holy, O Lord,
the fount of all holiness.
Holding his hands extended over the offerings, says:
Make holy, therefore, these gifts, we pray,
by sending down your Spirit upon them
like the dewfall,
so that they may become for us
the Body and Blood of our Lord, Jesus Christ.

Dew in Scripture refers to blessings and new life. In desert like areas dewfall is necessary to maintain vegetation. Figuratively it represents gentle freshness and fruitfulness.

"Let my teaching drop as the rain, My speech distill as the dew". (Deuteronomy 32:2).

"May God give you of the dew of heaven". (Genesis 27: 28).

At the time he was betrayed
and entered willingly into his Passion,
he took bread and, giving thanks, broke it,
and gave it to his disciples, saying ...

In a similar way, when supper was ended,
he took the chalice and, once more giving thanks,
he gave it to his disciples, saying ...

The words of consecration are the same in all of the Eucharistic Prayers.

Therefore, as we celebrate
the memorial of his Death and Resurrection,
we offer you, Lord,
the Bread of life and the Chalice of salvation,
giving thanks that you have held us worthy
to be in your presence and minister to you.

"I am the bread of life" (John 6:35-48).

"I will lift up the chalice of salvation and call on the name of the Lord". (Psalm 116:13).

Humbly we pray
that, partaking of the Body and Blood of Christ,
we may be gathered into one by the Holy Spirit.
Remember, Lord, your Church,
spread throughout the world,
and bring her to the fullness of charity,
together with N. our Pope and N. our Bishop
and all the clergy.

"The whole Catholic Church spread throughout the earth". (*St Polycarp*).

In Masses for the Dead, the following may be added:
Remember your servant N.,
whom you have called (today)

from this world to yourself.
Grant that he (she) who was united with your Son
in a death like his,
may also be one with him in his Resurrection.

"For if we have been united with him in a death like
his, we shall certainly be united with him in a resurrection
like his". (Romans 6:5).

Remember also our brothers and sisters
who have fallen asleep in the hope of the resurrection,
and all who have died in your mercy:
welcome them into the light of your face.

"They are happy ... who walk, O Lord, in the light of
your face". (Psalms 89:16).

Have mercy on us all, we pray,
that with the blessed Virgin Mary, Mother of God,
with the blessed Apostles,
and all the Saints who have pleased you
throughout the ages,
we may merit to be co-heirs to eternal life,
and may praise and glorify you
through your Son, Jesus Christ.

"Now if we are children, then we are heirs, heirs of
God and co-heirs with Christ, if indeed we share in his
sufferings in order that we may also share in his glory".
(Romans 8:17).

Eucharistic Prayer III

The third Eucharistic prayer is based on preliminary work by a holy Benedictine monk, Father Cyprian Vagaggini, and approved by Pope Paul VI, it blends together various biblical passages and ancient liturgical texts.

You are indeed Holy, O Lord,
and all you have created rightly gives you praise,
for through your Son our Lord Jesus Christ,
by the power and working of the Holy Spirit,
you give life to all things and make them holy,
and you never cease to gather a people to yourself,
so that from the rising of the sun to its setting
a pure sacrifice may be offered to your name.

"From the rising of the sun to its setting, praised be the name of the Lord". (Psalms 113:3).

"From the rising of the sun to its setting, my name is great among the nations; Incense offerings are made to my name everywhere, and a pure offering; For my name is great among the nations, says the Lord of hosts". (Malachi 1:11).

He extends his hands over the offerings and says:
Therefore, O Lord, we humbly implore you:

by the same Spirit graciously make holy
these gifts we have brought to you for consecration,
that they may become the Body and Blood
of your Son our Lord Jesus Christ,
at whose command we celebrate these mysteries.

The Church implores the power of the Holy Spirit that the gifts offered by human hands be consecrated, that is, become Christ's Body and Blood, and that the spotless Victim to be received in Communion be for the salvation of those who will partake of it.

For on the night he was betrayed
he himself took bread,
and giving you thanks he said the blessing,
broke the bread and gave it to his disciples, saying ...

In a similar way, when supper was ended,
he took the chalice,
and giving you thanks he said the blessing,
and gave the chalice to his disciples, saying ...

Therefore, O Lord, as we celebrate
the memorial of the saving Passion of your Son,
his wondrous Resurrection and Ascension into heaven,
and as we look forward to his second coming,
we offer you in thanksgiving
this holy and living sacrifice.

The Church, fulfilling the command that she received from Christ the Lord through the Apostles, keeps the memorial of Christ, recalling especially his blessed Passion, glorious Resurrection, and Ascension into heaen.

Look, we pray, upon the oblation of your Church
and, recognizing the sacrificial Victim by whose death
you willed to reconcile us to yourself,
grant that we, who are nourished
by the Body and Blood of your Son
and filled with his Holy Spirit,
may become one body, one spirit in Christ.

In this very memorial, the Church, gathered here, offers in the Holy Spirit the spotless Victim to the Father. The Church's intention, however, is that the faithful not only offer this spotless Victim but also learn to offer themselves, and so day by day to be consummated, through Christ the Mediator, into unity with God and with each other, so that at last God may be all in all.

May he make of us an eternal offering to you,
so that we may obtain an inheritance with your elect,
especially with the most blessed Virgin Mary,
Mother of God,
with your blessed Apostles and glorious Martyrs
(with Saint N.: the Saint of the day or Patron Saint)
and with all the Saints,

on whose constant intercession in your presence
we rely for unfailing help.

"Blessed be the God and Father of our Lord Jesus Christ, who in his great mercy gave us a new birth to a living hope through the resurrection of Jesus Christ from the dead, to an inheritance that is imperishable, undefiled, and unfading, kept in heaven for you". (1 Peter 1:3-4).

May this Sacrifice of our reconciliation,
we pray, O Lord,
advance the peace and salvation of all the world.
Be pleased to confirm in faith and charity
your pilgrim Church on earth,
with your servant N. our Pope and N. our Bishop,
the Order of Bishops, all the clergy,
and the entire people you have gained for your own.

Prayer for the whole Church was important for the first Christian communities. Saint Polycarp shortly before his death in the year 156 prayed aloud for"for all who were know to him and for the whole Catholic Church spread throughout the earth".

"The people whom I formed for myself, that they might recount my praise". (Isaiah 43:21).

"A people of his own" (1 Peter 2:9)

Listen graciously to the prayers of this family,
whom you have summoned before you:

in your compassion, O merciful Father,
gather to yourself all your children
scattered throughout the world.

The Eucharist is always celebrated in communion with
the entire Church, of heaven as well as of earth, and that
the offering is made for her and for all her members,
living and dead, who have been called to participate in the
redemption and the salvation purchased by Christ's Body
and Blood.

† To our departed brothers and sisters
and to all who were pleasing to you
at their passing from this life,
give kind admittance to your kingdom.
There we hope to enjoy for ever
the fullness of your glory
through Christ our Lord,
through whom you bestow on the world
all that is good. †

In Masses for the Dead, the following may be said:
† Remember your servant N.
whom you have called (today)
from this world to yourself.
Grant that he (she) who was united with your Son
in a death like his,
may also be one with him in his Resurrection,

when from the earth
he will raise up in the flesh those who have died,
and transform our lowly body
after the pattern of his own glorious body.
To our departed brothers and sisters, too,
and to all who were pleasing to you at their passing from this l
give kind admittance to your kingdom.
There we hope to enjoy for ever
the fullness of your glory,
when you will wipe away every tear from our eyes.
For seeing you, our God, as you are,
we shall be like you for all the ages
and praise you without end,
through Christ our Lord,
through whom you bestow on the world all that is good. †

"For if we have been united with him in a death like
his, we shall certainly be united with him in a resurrection like
his". (Romans 6:5).

"God will wipe away every tear from their eyes".
(Revelation 7:17).

"He will wipe every tear from their eyes".
(Revelation 21:3-4).

Eucharistic Prayer IV

The fourth Eucharistic prayer is based on the "Anaphora of St. Basil". St. Basil was born in 330 in Caesarea of Cappodocia in the eastern Mediterranean. After he was made Bishop of Caesarea, he wrote a Eucharistic prayer according to the traditional form.

It is truly right to give you thanks,
truly just to give you glory, Father most holy,
for you are the one God living and true,
existing before all ages and abiding for all eternity,
dwelling in unapproachable light;

"Who alone has immortality and dwells in unapproachable light". (1 Timothy 6:16).
"God is light and in him is no darkness at all".
(1 John 1:5).

yet you, who alone are good, the source of life,
have made all that is,
so that you might fill your creatures with blessings
and bring joy to many of them
by the glory of your light.
And so, in your presence are countless hosts of Angels,
who serve you day and night

and, gazing upon the glory of your face,
glorify you without ceasing.
With them we, too, confess your name in exultation,
giving voice to every creature under heaven
as we acclaim:
Holy, Holy, Holy Lord God of hosts...
We give you praise, Father most holy,
for you are great,
and you have fashioned all your works
in wisdom and in love.
You formed man in your own image
and entrusted the whole world to his care,
so that in serving you alone, the Creator,
he might have dominion over all creatures.

"God said, "Let us make man in our image, after our
likeness. Let them have dominion over ... all the creatures
... on the earth". (Genesis 1:26).

And when through disobedience
he had lost your friendship,
you did not abandon him to the domain of death.
For you came in mercy to the aid of all,
so that those who seek might find you.
Time and again you offered them covenants
and through the prophets
taught them to look forward to salvation.

"Then as one man's trespass led to condemnation for all men, so one man's act of righteousness leads to acquittal and life for all men. For as by one man's disobedience many were made sinners, so by one man's obedience many will be made righteous. Law came in, to increase the trespass; but where sin increased, grace abounded all the more". (Romans 5:18-20).

And you so loved the world, Father most holy,
that in the fullness of time
you sent your Only Begotten Son to be our Saviour.

"But when the fullness of time had come, God sent his Son, born of a woman, born under the Law". (Galatians 4:4).

Made incarnate by the Holy Spirit
and born of the Virgin Mary,
he shared our human nature
in all things but sin.

"For we do not have a high priest who is unable to sympathize with our weaknesses, but one who has similarly been tested in every way, yet without sin". (Hebrews 4:15).

To the poor he proclaimed the good news of salvation,
to prisoners, freedom,
and to the sorrowful of heart, joy.

"The Spirit of the Lord is upon me, because he has anointed me to bring glad tidings to the poor. He has sent me to proclaim liberty to captives and recovery of sight to the blind, to let the oppressed go free". (Luke 4:18).

To accomplish your plan,
he gave himself up to death,
and, rising from the dead,
he destroyed death and restored life.

"Our Saviour, Christ Jesus, who has destroyed death and has brought life". (2 Timothy 1:10).

And that we might live no longer for ourselves
but for him who died and rose again for us,
he sent the Holy Spirit from you, Father,
as the first fruits for those who believe,
so that, bringing to perfection his work in the world,
he might sanctify creation to the full.

"He indeed died for all, so that those who live might no longer live for themselves but for him who for their sake died and was raised". (2 Corinthians 5:15).

"We ourselves, who have the first fruits of the Spirit, groan inwardly as we wait for adoption as sons, the redemption of our bodies". (Romans 8:23).

He extends his hands over the offerings and says:
Therefore, O Lord, we pray:

may this same Holy Spirit
graciously sanctify these offerings,
that they may become
the Body and Blood of our Lord Jesus Christ
for the celebration of this great mystery,
which he himself left us as an eternal covenant.

"My covenant will be ... an everlasting covenant".
(Genesis 17:13).

For when the hour had come
for him to be glorified by you, Father most holy,
having loved his own who were in the world,
he loved them to the end:
and while they were at supper,
he took bread, blessed and broke it,
and gave it to his disciples, saying ...

"Having loved his own who were in the world, he
loved them to the end."(John 13).

It was just in this manner that Jesus loved on that last
evening. He loved his "own", those who were then with
him, and all those who were to inherit the mystery from
them.

The words we repeat when we celebrate the Eucharist,
are precisely the revelation of this love through which,
once and for all, for all time and until the end of the ages,
he shared himself! Even before giving himself on the

cross, as the "Lamb who takes away the sins of the world", he shared himself as food and drink: bread and wine, so that "they may have life, and have it abundantly" (John 10:10). It was thus that he "loved to the end". (*Blessed John Paul II*).

In a similar way,
taking the chalice filled with the fruit of the vine,

"I tell you, from now on I shall not drink this fruit of the vine until the day when I drink it with you new in the kingdom of my Father". (Matthew 26:2).

he gave thanks, and gave the chalice to his disciples,
saying ...

Therefore, O Lord,
as we now celebrate the memorial of our redemption,
we remember Christ's death
and his descent to the realm of the dead,
we proclaim his Resurrection
and his Ascension to your right hand;
and as we await his coming in glory,
we offer you his Body and Blood,
the sacrifice acceptable to you
which brings salvation to the whole world.

"For the grace of God has appeared, bringing salvation for all people". (Titus 2:11).

Look, O Lord, upon the Sacrifice
which you yourself have provided for your Church,
and grant in your loving kindness
to all who partake of this one Bread and one Chalice
that, gathered into one body by the Holy Spirit,
they may truly become a living sacrifice in Christ
to the praise of your glory.

"The cup of blessing that we bless, is it not a participation in the blood of Christ? The bread that we break, is it not a participation in the body of Christ? Because there is one bread, we who are many are one body, for we all partake of the one bread". (1 Corinthians 10:16-17).

"Present your bodies as a living sacrifice, holy and acceptable to God, which is your spiritual worship". (Romans 12:1).

"To the praise of his glory". (Eph 1:12).

Therefore, Lord, remember now
all for whom we offer this sacrifice:
especially your servant, N. our Pope,
N. our Bishop, and the whole Order of Bishops,
all the clergy, those who take part in this offering,
those gathered here before you,
your entire people,
and all who seek you with a sincere heart.

Remember also those who have died
in the peace of your Christ
and all the dead, whose faith you alone have known.

"The Lord knows those who are his". (2 Timothy 2:19).

To all of us, your children,
grant, O merciful Father,
that we may enter into a heavenly inheritance
with the blessed Virgin Mary, Mother of God,
and with your Apostles and Saints in your kingdom.
There, with the whole of creation,
freed from the corruption of sin and death,
may we glorify you through Christ our Lord,
through whom you bestow on the world
all that is good.

"Creation itself will be set free from its bondage to corruption and obtain the glorious liberty of the children of God". (Romans 8:21).

"An inheritance which is imperishable". (1 Peter 1:4).

The Communion Rite

The Lord's Prayer

"The Lord's Prayer is truly the summary of the whole Gospel". (*Tertullian*).

At the Saviour's command
and formed by divine teaching,
we dare to say:

In response to his disciples' request "Lord, teach us to pray" (Luke 11:1), Jesus commanded them to pray the great Christian prayer, the Our Father. "Simple and faithful trust, humble and joyous assurance are the proper dispositions for one who prays the Our Father". (Cf. CCC n. 2797).

Our Father, who art in heaven,
hallowed be thy name;
thy kingdom come,
thy will be done
on earth as it is in heaven.
Give us this day our daily bread,
and forgive us our trespasses,
as we forgive those who trespass against us;

and lead us not into temptation,
but deliver us from evil.

"The Lord's Prayer is the most perfect of prayers. ... In it we ask, not only for all the things we can rightly desire, but also in the sequence that they should be desired. This prayer not only teaches us to ask for things, but also in what order we should desire them". (*St Thomas Aquinas*).

Deliver us, Lord, we pray, from every evil,
graciously grant peace in our days,
that, by the help of your mercy,
we may be always free from sin
and safe from all distress,
as we await the blessed hope
and the coming of our Saviour, Jesus Christ.

"Awaiting our blessed hope, the appearing of the glory of our great God and Saviour Jesus Christ". (Titus 2: 13).

For the kingdom,
the power and the glory are yours
now and for ever.

The acclamation "For the kingdom, the power and the glory are yours, now and forever," takes up "the first three petitions to our Father: the glorification of his name, the coming of his reign, and the power of his saving will. But these prayers are now proclaimed as adoration and thanksgiving, as in the liturgy of heaven. The ruler of this world has mendaciously attributed to himself the three titles of kingship, power, and glory. Christ, the Lord, restores them to his Father and our Father, until he hands over the kingdom to him when the mystery of salvation will be brought to its completion and God will be all in all." (CCC n. 2855).

Lord Jesus Christ,
who said to your Apostles,
Peace I leave you, my peace I give you,
look not on our sins,
but on the faith of your Church,
and graciously grant her peace and unity
in accordance with your will.
Who live and reign for ever and ever.
Amen.

"Peace I leave with you; my peace I give to you". (John 14:27).

"Peace makers who sow in peace reap a harvest of righteousness". (James 4:17-18).

The peace of the Lord be with you always. (cf. John 16:33; 20:19, 21, 26).
And with your spirit.

Let us offer each other the sign of peace.

The sign of peace

When the ministers reached the altar Bishop Priest and Deacon they kiss the altar. After the reading of the Gospel the Deacon or the Priest kisses the Gospel book and before holy Communion the exchange the sign all the kiss of peace. The altar is kissed because it has been consecrated by the invocation of the Holy Spirit. The Gospel book is kissed because of through the power of the spirit Christ is present in the assembly when his word is proclaimed. We show a sign of reverence to our neighbour because as Saint Paul tells us body is the temple of the Holy Spirit. And so we conclude that the kiss in the liturgy is a sign of the Holy Spirit and has nothing to do with any human connotations of goodwill or friendship. The reason why so many have been dissatisfied with the sign of peace is because it has not been seen as a sacred action but rather as a sign of fellowship. Fellowship is not lacking but follows upon the action of the Spirit that we might be one body one spirit it in Christ.

"It should be kept in mind that nothing is lost when the sign of peace is marked by a sobriety which preserves the proper spirit of the celebration, as, for example, when it is restricted to one's immediate neighbours". (*Sacramentum caritatis n. 49*).

The Fraction, the "Breaking of the Bread"

"They recognized him in the breaking of bread". (cf. Luke 24:35).

"The 'breaking of bread' as the Eucharist was called in earliest times, has always been at the centre of the Church's life. Through it Christ makes present within time the mystery of his death and resurrection. In it he is received in person as the 'living bread come down from heaven' (John 6:51), and with him we receive the pledge of eternal life and a foretaste of the eternal banquet of the heavenly Jerusalem". (*Blessed John Paul II*).

The celebrant takes the host, breaks it over the paten, and places a small piece in the chalice, saying quietly:

May this mingling of the Body and Blood
of our Lord Jesus Christ
bring eternal life to us who receive it.

Lamb of God

This ancient practice is found in the liturgies of both the East and West. It is a direct preparation for the reception of the Body and Blood of the Lord. The sacrifice has been offered and now it is to be shared.

Our earthly gifts are returned to us as heavenly food. The mingling of the two Species reminds us that we are destined to participate in the divinity and immortality of Christ won for us by his Passion, death and Resurrection.

The hymn *Lamb of God, you take away the sins of the world, have mercy on us* was introduced by Pope Sergius (687-701) to accompany the Fraction (breaking of the bread) and was repeated as long as the Fraction was taking place. It is concluded with the words *grant us peace*.

After agreeing to baptize him along with the sinners, John the Baptist looked at Jesus and pointed him out as the "Lamb of God, who takes away the sin of the world". By doing so, he reveals that Jesus is at the same time the suffering Servant who silently allows himself to be led to the slaughter and who bears the sin of the multitudes, and also the Paschal Lamb, the symbol of Israel's redemption at the first Passover. Christ's whole life expresses his mission: "to serve, and to give his life as a ransom for many. (CCC 608); (cf. John 1:29, 36; cf. Rev 5:6-13; 22:1-3).

The following prayers for forgiveness are recited quietly:

Lord Jesus Christ, Son of the living God,
who by the will of the Father
and the work of the Holy Spirit,
through your Death gave life to the world;
free me by this, your most holy Body and Blood,
from all my sins and from every evil;
keep me always faithful to your commandments,
and never let me be parted from you.

May the receiving of your Body and Blood, Lord Jesus
Christ, not bring me to judgment and condemnation, but
through your loving mercy be for me protection in mind
and body, and a healing remedy.

Behold the Lamb of God, behold him who takes away
the sins of the world. Blessed are those called to the
supper of the Lamb.

"Blessed are those who have been called to the
wedding feast of the Lamb". (Revelation 19: 9).

"Behold the Lamb of God" a direct reference to the
words of Saint John the Baptist. The previous text "This
is the Lamb of God" is restrictive in its meaning whereas
the word "Behold" is both immediate and timeless. It was
the role of John the Baptist to point out the Lord's
Anointed when He came, and John continues his mission
until the Lord comes again at the end of time.

And together with the people he adds once:
Lord, I am not worthy that you should enter under my
roof, but only say the word and my soul shall be healed.

At this most sacred moment of Communion the
Church puts on our lips, not the words of a great saint or
mystic but those of a pagan soldier who showed great
faith and trust in the Lord and took that vital first step of
inviting him into his life. (Matthew 8: 5-13).

The Priest says quietly:
May the Body of Christ
keep me safe for eternal life.

Then he takes the chalice and says quietly:
May the Blood of Christ
keep me safe for eternal life.

Holy Communion may be received in the hand or on the tongue. At the beginning of the fourth century Saint Cyril of Jerusalem told his congregation, "When you approach, do not extend your hands with palms upward and fingers apart, but make your left hand a throne for your right hand, since the latter is to receive the King".

The Priest raises a host slightly and shows it to each of the communicants, saying:

The Body of Christ.
Amen.

Saint Ambrose (337-397) wrote, "not without reason do you say 'Amen', for you acknowledge in your heart that you are receiving the body of Christ. When you present yourself, the priest says to you, 'the body of Christ', and you reply 'Amen' that is,' it is so'. Let the heart persevere in what the tongue confesses".

The Curé d'Ars, Saint John Mary Vianney, used to tell his parishioners: "Come to communion ... It is true that you are not worthy of it, but you need it".

While he carries out the purification, the Priest says quietly:
What has passed our lips as food, O Lord,
may we possess in purity of heart,
that what has been given to us in time
may be our healing for eternity.

The Priest may return to the chair. If appropriate, a sacred silence may be observed for a while, or a psalm or other canticle of praise or a hymn may be sung. Then, standing at the altar or at the chair and facing the people, with hands joined, the Priest says: Let us pray.

The prayer after communion is one of petition that the graces of the holy Eucharist may be effective in us and that we may live out the mystery of love which we have celebrated. "You have become one body, so be what you are, loving one another, keeping the same faith, the same hope, an undivided charity". *Saint Augustine*

All pray in silence with the Priest for a while, unless silence has just been observed. Then the Priest, with hands extended, says the Prayer after Communion, at the end of which the people acclaim: *Amen.*

The Concluding Rites

The Blessing and dismissal

The blessing at the end of Mass was originally only given by the Pope or other bishops. Then in the 12th and 13th century ordinary priests were allowed to give it.

In the Liturgy the word "dismissal" has come to imply a "mission".

The Eucharist and mission

"The love that we celebrate in the sacrament is not something we can keep to ourselves. By its very nature it demands to be shared with all. What the world needs is God's love; it needs to encounter Christ and to believe in him. The Eucharist is thus the source and summit not only of the Church's life, but also of her mission: 'an authentically Eucharistic Church is a missionary Church.' We too must tell our brothers and sisters with conviction: 'That which we have seen and heard we proclaim also to you, so that you may have fellowship with us' (1 John 1:3). Truly, nothing is more beautiful than to know Christ and to make him known to others". (*Pope Benedict XVI*).

After the blessing, the deacon or the priest dismisses the people with one of the following:

Go forth, the Mass is ended.

Pope Benedict XVI recently added the following three texts at the request of the Synod of Bishops.

Go and announce the Gospel of the Lord.
Go in peace, glorifying the Lord by your life.
Go in peace.

From Mass to "mission"

"Receiving the Bread of Life, the disciples of Christ ready themselves to undertake with the strength of the Risen Lord and his Spirit the tasks which await them in their ordinary life. For the faithful who have understood the meaning of what they have done, the Eucharistic celebration does not stop at the church door. Like the first witnesses of the Resurrection, Christians who gather each Sunday to experience and proclaim the presence of the Risen Lord are called to evangelize and bear witness in their daily lives. Given this, the Prayer after Communion and the Concluding Rite – the Final Blessing and the Dismissal – need to be better valued and appreciated, so that all who have shared in the Eucharist may come to a deeper sense of the responsibility which is entrusted to them. Once the assembly disperses, Christ's disciples return to their everyday surroundings with the commitment to make their whole life a gift, a spiritual sacrifice pleasing to God (cf. Romans 12:1). They feel indebted to their brothers and sisters because of what they have received in the celebration, not unlike the disciples of Emmaus who, once they had recognized the Risen Christ "in the breaking of the bread" (cf. Luke 24:30-32), felt the need to return immediately to share with their brothers and sisters the joy of meeting the Lord (cf. Luke 24:33-35)". (*Blessed John Paul II*).

The Priest venerates the altar with a kiss, as at the beginning. After making a profound bow with the ministers, he withdraws.

Conclusion

The founder of the liturgical movement, Dom Prosper Guéranger, Abbot of Solesmes, often spoke of the importance of reading, meditating and praying the texts of the liturgy. He recognised the importance of scholarly study, but the Abbot believed that a greater and more profound knowledge could come from the study of liturgical books. This small work is designed to help the reader reflect upon the texts of the Order of Mass in order to enter more deeply in the celebration of the Mystery of Faith.

Endnote

[1] This greeting occurs frequently in the New Testament: 1 Corinthians 1:3, Romans 1: 7, 2 Corinthians 1: 2, Ephesians 1:2, Philippians 1:2, Philemon 1:3. A similar greeting can be found in other new Testament letters, Colossians 1:2, 1 Peter 1:2, 1 Timothy 1: 2, 2 Timothy 1: 2, Titus 1:4, 2 John 3, Revelation 1: 4.